THIS JOURNAL BELONGS TO

Made in the USA
Columbia, SC
11 December 2023

28398005R00065